W9-DET-973

STUBBORN CHILD

STUBBORN CHILD

POEMS BY Peter E. Murphy

To Robert,
From one stubborn
poet to another!

Peter E. [signature]
1 April 05

JANE STREET PRESS / NYC

2005

© 2005 Peter E. Murphy

ISBN 0-9723943-2-x

Jane Street Press
1 Jane Street, Suite 5F
New York, NY 10014
janestreet.com/press

Cover artwork: "Half Past Three (The Poet)" by Marc Chagall, 1911.
  Used by permission of the Philadelphia Museum of Art:
  The Louise and Walter Arensberg Collection, 1950.

Author's photo: Wayne Romanowski

Book & cover design: Douglas Goetsch, Louise Millmann

"The Stubborn Child" from The Complete Fairy Tales of the Brothers
Grimm by Jack Zipes, translator, © 1987 by Jack Zipes. Used by
permission of Bantam Books, a division of Random House, Inc.

I wish to thank the following who have looked after this stubborn poet and
helped show him a way home. Hubert Babinski, friend and first teacher,
First Thursday, the Getaway Gang at Ocean Grove for laughter and light,
and to generations of students who "have trod, have trod, have trod . . . ."

I am grateful to the following institutions whose grants and support helped
in the writing of these poems. The New Jersey Council for the Arts,
The Geraldine R. Dodge Foundation, especially Jim Haba and Scott McVay,
The Corporation of Yaddo, The Virginia Center for the Creative Arts, and
The Louhelen Bahá'í School.

Special thanks to Stephen Dunn for thirty years of friendship and mentor-
ing, to Douglas Goetsch for his support, generosity and genius, and to his
Jane Street Press for bringing this collection into print.

For Sonya and Amanda, without whom . . .

CONTENTS

The Stubborn Child

Once upon a time there was a stubborn child who never did what his mother told him to do. The dear Lord, therefore, did not look kindly upon him and let him become sick. No doctor could cure him, and in a short time, he lay on his deathbed. After he was lowered into his grave and was covered over with earth, one of his little arms suddenly emerged and reached up into the air. They pushed it back down and covered the earth with fresh earth, but that did not help. The little arm kept popping out. So the child's mother had to go to the grave herself and smack the little arm with a switch. After she had done that, the arm withdrew, and then, for the first time, the child had peace beneath the earth.

– The Brothers Grimm

1

The New Boy

Crossing Brooklyn Ferry from Staten Island
did not close the doors of the orphanage inside him.
On that boat he studied *Casper the Friendly Ghost*
and ate a hot dog and Coke, the first supper of a life
he hoped not to suffer.

Crossing the Halloween Narrows that seamed
the night as if it were a border, he hoped to please
this new family, please their mint blue car
that drove him to the ferry from the school
for boys that darkened when he needed light.

He inhaled the salt breeze and drank his Coke
and thought of the ghost that could not make friends
of the living by being what he was, which was dead.
He had to be heroic instead, the way little boys are not.
Where had Casper lived on Earth? he wondered.

How did he die? Why didn't he return to people
who loved him? He wondered too, if he would frighten
those who saw the deadness within him.
Is there a home where boys could learn to live
within their bodies? Where he could learn to live

in this new family? Would they keep him if he fails,
or throw him out to wander the streets of Brooklyn
begging for food or coins or love? Must he rattle
through these homes forever, pleading for someone
to play with, someone mean enough to take him in?

The Neighborhood

Remember the Wollachuck twins
who never said words but mumbled between them
a lumbering series of prime numbers that sounded
like air bubbles rising to the surface of the creek.
Remember the Wollachucks
who never used poles but dropped
a milk bottle filled with bread into shallow water.
And when they pulled it up, it was screaming
with bony, black killies, useless even for bait.
Remember how one tugged out a fish,
put its head into his mouth and bit down,
then gave it to his brother to chew the tail,
as they chomped through twenty or thirty
before squeezing out the salt water
and swallowing the bread.

As the current rolls in and breaks at my feet,
the Wollachucks rise out of the deepest waters
and slosh into shore. Their tongues sparkle,
licking the salt from their lips.
I cast my lure across the opaque surface.
It sinks until something strikes it and begins to fight back.
I reel in what can be reeled in, and the Wollachucks help me.
One scrapes its razor scales, hacks off its head and tail.
The other offers me its meat, and I will eat it.

Fishing

And for all this, nature is never spent;
There lives the dearest freshness deep down things.

– Hopkins

The year the mackerel made a run through Howard Beach
we dropped cherry bombs off the bridge,
taping them to rocks so they would sink quickly
before going off.

First a gale of bubbles—then a bouquet
of fishes would rise to the surface,
their white bellies rolling upwards

like large, bloodshot eyeballs. Everything
fleet or clumsy, no matter how deep,
coming up dead.

Oreo

When my Welsh mama died,
I was taken in by an aunt who worked
for you, who slipped tray after tray
of you into the cellophane bags
she sneaked home to wrap my lunch.
Everyday you were present in second grade,
two black eyes punched into the bleached
skin of my bologna and mustard sandwich.
How can I forgive you what you were?
How you troubled me for years until the old man
got a new wife who bought different cookies,
and made ham and lettuce and mayonnaise
and occasionally tomato.

I never looked back, though I loved that aunt
who took me from nuns that made me eat sweet
potatoes, even after I spilled my spew onto the plate
and made me eat that too. Sweet potatoes. How bitter,
and Oreos with their inner light flickering
from two dark lids, black and white, black and white
slapping me, yelling Eat it all! Eat it all!

Public Hell

Sin was not necessarily something that you did:
it might be something that happened to you.

– Orwell

At an early grade, I was switched in school from Catholic
to Public and thought they switched my religion as well.

I feared eternity in public hell which no one taught,
so terrible it must be, they could not mention it.

They hauled me out of Publics at the end of third,
turned me back to Catholic for the Fifth.

I lost a year or gained one, I didn't know. It wasn't
that I was a genius who didn't need his Fourth—

Columbus discovered America and stuff, I knew,
but didn't know what drove him or why

they kept me there a second year. True, I passed
my courses and coursed the hallways on an errand,

always with a pass. He'll be back again next year,
I heard them say, to catch up with his class.

And I was—a dumb bunny, a repeater,
someone good to post from nun to nun,

a small slip of paper in his hand. "Send the boy,"
the note said. "It doesn't matter."

The Bridge

Unspeakable, the noise under that bridge
as we sat on a bulkhead, opened our flies
and pulled out our small peckers.

There was tons we didn't know, could hardly imagine.
How that curved flabbiness, in love
with its own indifference until things got serious,
could grow majestic and tough
before our eyes.
How someone started dreaming and humming,
chanting a song we all picked up
in our up and down movements.

We sat on a ledge looking over the deep channel,
the ferocious current slapping the concrete columns.
We chanted louder and louder, filling the cavern
with music.

Learning to Swim at Poverty Beach

A few yards out the drop
dropped fifty feet into darkness
dredged for submarines and spider crabs
whose intricate webs, I imagined,
would wrap around my feet
and pull me under.
At night on the damp sand older boys
laid down their girls who let them
go deep, coming up weak, soggy,
and out of breath.

This was years before I realized
how stupid I was, and lucky.
Years before the draft board leveled
the neighborhood, before Walter Wetzel
took his famous last jump shot,
before Becker and O'Leary and Roe
and San Fillipo doped themselves
into graves so shallow, I swear I saw them
shooting up again on Cross Bay Boulevard.
This was years before I noticed
how car lights crossing Jamaica Bay
could turn the dark, dirty water
into something almost beautiful.

Milo

I was fifteen the summer I grew tired
of being a kid. I wasn't very good at it.
None of my clothes fit, and I couldn't
pronounce the vocabulary of hanging out,
even at Milo's Clam Bar where I worked
off the books for overpriced cans of beer.
Milo never bothered to get a liquor license
so he wasn't afraid of losing it. He served
anyone who came up with fifty cents a can
he paid a quarter for. His place buzzed
with teenagers rubbing together their coins
to chug half a Rheingold or Schlitz.
Milo liked to touch the girls, and his girlfriend
didn't mind until his wife caught up with her
and poked her with a knife.
He tried to teach me how to ease a blade
between the tight lips of a littleneck,
and I practiced but could not get it to open
its bright mouth. My hands at the end of a lesson
were bloodied from trying, stinging, the fishy smell
clinging to me the way no girl would.
So I swept the patio, helped out on the dock.
One day a cabin cruiser pulled up.
I caught the rope tossed by a young goddess,
felt it tighten around my thin fingers as I looped
it to a pole and felt the whole world shiver
from the wake of a speedboat when she walked by,
followed by parents and a dog, up the gangplank
to where Milo stood on the deck shucking
his way through his customers, his one hand
clutching the hard shell of a cherrystone,
the other flicking the dull edge of the knife
until a moist tongue emerged which he sucked
into his own mouth and swallowed in one gulp.

Underemployment

There was nothing I could do to get myself
fired from a small machine shop
in the middle of Brooklyn.
I came in late, left early, showed up drunk—
Nothing worked.

No matter how many details I botched,
usually on purpose, the boss wouldn't can me.
He was so patient I wanted to slap him
with a wrench.

I thought I finally had him when I stuck my hand
into a sink of muric acid.
He hauled me out, sloshed me with water,
and when he was done screaming,
said softly I'd be okay, told me to be more careful.

You know those signs that brag how many days
without an accident? He took his down,
put up a calendar with a view of mountains
most people in Brooklyn would never see.

Finally, I stopped showing up, stayed on the BMT
crossing into Manhattan under the busy streets
where so much work was getting done.

I rode each day to the end of the line,
then back again, passing below the shop
where he paced by the time clock, lifting my blank card
from its metal slot, rubbing it with his calloused fingers,
replacing it as I dove deeper and deeper, punching in
beneath the shiftless ground.

Sequence

First

Standing in her basement
pressing her

against a door
all the years

of anticipation
beating their wings

inside me
before she could

show me
what to do

Second

She kissed
what had never
been kissed

And I could
only kiss
her back

Third

We drove around
looking
for a place
to park

until we turned
that corner
and found
a lot

with many
empty spaces
each needing
to be filled

The Judgment

I made love to a girl once, in Bristol,
tangling on the floor of the room she shared
with a guy who was absurdly depressed.
His left ear was mangled, looked
like a piece of dough.
He stared at his chess set for hours,
eating cold soup out of the tin can.

She was a young girl, fresh as a stream.
I don't remember how we met, how we got
on that floor together, our bodies slapping
the linoleum in a regular heartbeat.
I do remember thinking of her depressed guy
listening to our love grunts all night
with his one good ear.

She was giddy the next morning taking
her pill, making plans—she thought
I was staying. The guy sat in his chair
holding a rook. I told her Bristol
was a place to stop between Cardiff
and London, that I had to go,
that I would write.

She spent too much time in the bathroom,
her pain so jagged it sliced
through her paper skin.
She was lucky she didn't know to cut
the artery lengthwise.
I figured I should stay, give them a hand
to the hospital, clean up.
Instead I left.

The Narrows

for my mother

Out under the dark Verrazano
ocean ships pass from a thin body
of water to a wider one.
Before it, the statue of a woman
is being renovated, her new copper chest
already tarnished by urine
from the workmen who could have held it in.

Here, the lights from speeding cars
twist our shadows out of shape
and send them rushing ahead
to where my father and I will walk
as he finally says what killed you.
I had been told as a child, Cigarettes . . . Cancer,
and I pictured your lungs blacker
than the gritty coal miners of the Welsh valley
we were born in.

Instead, he tells me how you drowned yourself,
and I am pulled into that river of sadness
that loosened the grip of your fingers.
You drowned yourself—it rushes through my life
rising and flooding the narrow land
on which I walk between your death and mine.

The Stubborn Child

after Grimm

His mother had taken him into her grave
where he continued to fidget. Quiet down,
she yelled, or we'll get no peace here too.
But his arms kept lifting and falling
and his legs moved back and forth in perpetual dance.

The boy wanted to please his mother who loved him,
who always gave him the best of what she had.
But he could not find comfort in her grave
and continued to maunder through those sleepless years,
his skinny chest surging as if it were still a home to breath.

You're not dead yet, are you little boy? she screamed
and smacked him with her bony hand and chased him
with a kitchen knife around their small compartment.
She shoved him with her thin right arm so hard
he popped right out of the grave

he had been trying to live in, and lay weak,
half blind and covered with earth.
The dead smells on his skin made the small boy dizzy.
When he tried to walk, he fell, and he cried
each day for years to live without stumbling.

He does not mention any of this to his daughter
who sleeps her stubborn sleep each night
as he stands in her room and prays through her
restless years, waving his arms above her,
sweeping and stirring the immaculate air.

Heavy Construction

Some nights looking for my father
I'd drive downtown near Wall Street
and double park outside The Market,
Keatons, The Blarney Cafe—my warning
lights flashing—and dig through bankrupt men
wasted from their afternoon cocktails.

One night too late, I found him Midtown
drinking Manhattans. He insisted
I meet his good friend the bartender
who poured and stirred and served us
one for the road.

My father, who was as shy with strangers
as he was with his own children,
introduced me that night
as his smart son who quit school
to write poetry and crack cement
with a jackhammer. He handed me
a twenty to drive him home, passed out
before we got there.

Too late to sleep after getting him
inside, I took a shot, showered and drove
back out as the sun was rising.
A new job that day, a new place to break
open the earth, to pull out the dirt,
start over.

Why I Am Not a Catholic

I practiced communion for months, kneeling
at a cracked marble altar, my hands corrected by nuns
who squeezed my fingers into little shriveled wings,
turning them upward toward the starry ceiling
before laying a candy wafer on my tongue.
I prayed to the Virgin's statue that looked down
in plaster silence, her bare feet crushing a snake's body
against a globe of the world.

Later, I was anointed by the priest
who wrestled me to the floor of the sacristy
and rubbed his hands over my body.
He massaged them into the joints of my spine,
pressed them into the muscles of my legs,
and stroked the soft flesh of my soul
which grew hard when he touched it, then died.

Nights, I knelt against my bed, reading psalms
aloud, chanting the dark words that flowed through me
like cold blood until you heard my wailing,
loved me for my sins and offered me your breast.
I did not believe I would ever come back to life,
but when you touched me and I rose toward heaven,
I was filled with tongues and could speak
for the first time the language of the living,
which gushed out of me in one intelligible voice,
ancient and beautiful.

Baptism

This time I wake under a bridge.
My ochre face rises in the rear
view mirror like a jaundiced sun.
This time my trousers are damp.
This time my trousers are dry.
This time I wake in a gutter.
Rain flows around me.

This time I am alone.
This time I am alone.
This time it is a river.
This time an inlet.
Waters rush through me.
A disorganized river.
This proof.

This time I wake in the Chevy.
My salmon face rises in the mirror.
This time an ocean.
The days crash over me.
My name is *Not Yet*.
My name is *Almost*.
My name is *About to*.

2

Shaping Up

*... a method of selecting a work crew
from an assembled group of those available.*

1. The Hustlers

It's summer, 6:30 a.m. walking down 14th Street
to the union hall as the neighborhood gets up
for work every morning for a month. Sweet Lady
smiles, her rouged cheeks a dark sunrise, offers
me a kiss, asks me if I want a date. Nervous,
I say no thanks it's too early for me.
It's never too early, she says, for a good time.
But I am young and keep on going, two dollars
in my pocket for tokens and lunch—
hey man, Hey Man, HEY MAN as I'm walking by.
His skin brown-burnt and shiny, his arms flying
around like long sleeved jets, flapping his hands
as his sweet-dirty odor hits my face.
I need some money man, Sweet B'jesus man, just
a smell, a taste, and he Sweet B'jesuses me out
of my two dollars. And Jesus! at the hall I get
the nod from the guardian angel delegate who
calls me in and gives me a job in the Bronx.
I borrow a dollar and catch the IRT and make
the shift and pull and push my donkey-hoist levers
hoisting mortar and blocks to the top
of the scaffold, making more money in a week
than my grandfather made in a month when they used
Irishmen to haul bricks up ladders before replacing them
with gas machines.

There is something that is hard to talk about,
hard to get at, but it keeps pressing me,
lifting me to the tops of buildings where
I throw myself off every day of my life as I piss
away my nights drinking beer at college pubs,
looking for a girl who will hold me till I drop.

Winter comes before she does and the jobs slow
and stop coming, and I never move out of the hall
where gray men in coveralls with the news
in their laps, talk and smoke and drink
endless cups of coffee looking at the fat men
in business suits in the inner office wait for the phones
to ring, and I quit because there isn't enough
work to keep me going.

2. Eddie

I get a job fixing things at a night club and work
with a guy named Eddie who is ancient,
simple and has little hair and fewer teeth
and is too pickled most days to notice how shitty
his job is. We drink beer all day as he stands
in one spot washing the same acre of floor
for an hour. He can't read and can't write and one day
I send him, as a joke, to the bank next door
with a stick up note.
The teller touches a button and silent alarms go off,
but the guard knows Eddie for years and brings him back
and gives me hell for trouble and for laughing.
Eddie, drinking another beer in the back room,
grabs his mop and swabs his floor and squabbles
through toothless anger how I ain't ought to of done
that, how he ought to quit, how it ain't right
when a man's trying to make a living, to make
a fool out of him where he works. Eddie wants
to open his own bar in the neighborhood
and call it "Cocktail Lounge" and draw the tap
to a keg of never-ending beer and have someone
else mop up after him every day.

I get to work one morning, my head blocked,
my skin yellow from vodka, my tongue swollen,
choking me, making me want to throw up
at the smell of the liquors on the gantry
behind the bar. I call for Eddie to get some coffee.

He doesn't come, unlike him to hesitate
for get yourself a cup and keep the change,
probably shuffling his mop through his liquid
stupor as I sit through mine. I find him collapsed
in the back room with his head red-sticky
like a broken bottle of grenadine syrup, the burglar
gone, too frightened to know he killed an idiot.
I call the boss and the cops, then puke myself
sore, and I can't get up to unlock the door
to let them in. Later, after a shot or two of vodka,
my stomach settles and the hell in my head
freezes over.

3. The Dancer

I work my way out of the day shift, out of repairs,
and work the bar at night and the customers
and a girl or two as well, but not as many
as you'd think. We meet in another bar
when I bump her with my drink, and she gets
pissed and pours hers on my head, she tells
me later. Thick thighs and small breasts she gets
from ballet, gymnastics—she is choreographed
crazy as a child into an addict released from Creedmore
with half a liver. She dances topless
in go go bars where guys buy overpriced beers
and watch her kick and spin and move in ways
that get them hard. She dances on the bar
with an air conditioned mirror image above
the outstretched hands of the men holding
their stiff dollars, pushing their rolled up bills
into her bikini bottom that glitters all night
long, even as they remember her movements
with their wives at home in bed.

We live together and she's sleeping around
I know, but never catch her, never get her
to admit it. And one morning I'm called to Bellevue
to pick her up. She's raped crazy—

Some guy she meets the night before. I leave
her every week for good, but she says love,
and I think this love is terrible, hardly better
than none at all. So I stay another week,
each week, and drink vodka clear as water
and scentless on my breath so I don't know.
And sometimes I lose a day—once almost a week—
go out for a drink after hours and wake a few days
later, exhausted and yellow, not knowing
where I'd been, what I'd done, who I was with.
A drink in my hand—then blank—I wake up naked
in sunlight out on a neighbor's lawn grinding
my penis into the earth. I can't come and can't walk
and drag my pale legs through the grass,
hoist myself over the edge of the knee-high
kiddie pool, scraping my belly, spilling water
till the metal lip springs back, reforming
itself as I lie beneath the chlorine cold
which burns my eyes and nose till I gag
and rise above the surface.

4. Jasmine

I leave finally, and leave the bar and leave
the country and go to Wales for a week or two,
to see where I was born. I stay a year and live
in a Cardiff row house with Welsh kids who sign
on every week for the dole, pick up their pounds
and trade them in for drugs, and sit in laughter
and stupor and crashing out listening to Wishbone
Ash and "Retribution" and *I can't ball 'cause I got
the clap* . . . . We sleep in shifts, three bedrooms
cramped with lice and crabs and DDT from the clinic
where they shave our pubics and give us flyers
on hygiene and V.D.

One night there is a riot when Gypsy Blood freaks
on a girl named Jasmine and too much acid
and smashes windows with the electric guitar

he plays without plugging in. Crazy Steve gets hurt
getting in the way, and I feint and block the guitar
and knock Gypsy down and sit on him all night
while Charlie and Trevor and Twiz talk him down,
bring him in, and he lands.
Jasmine is 16, run away from Arab brothers
who promise her to a desert husband she's never met.
The brothers are slim sharp like switchblades
and know we have her and come around questioning
and dangerous.

I smuggle her out to another part of Cardiff
where we sleep one night on the floor of the house
of a friend. His mother smiles, thinking
we are lovers and tells us of her love for men
now dead and brings us blankets and hot tea
and leaves us alone for the night. I have a cold.
My nose drips like acid and I sniffle. My head
is clogged with mucus and with smoke lying
with Jasmine on the winter rug in front of the coal fire,
her dark voice and dark hair heavy in the air
like soot. I keep repeating myself, I realize,
the same crap over and over, each time a different girl,
a different drink, vodka or beer. I want
her fiercely and see myself swinging guitars,
breaking windows in my mind and bleeding
and falling to the ground. She knows she's leaving,
knows I'm not going with her and touches
my arm and turns away. I listen to the coals
hiss hot all night till the cold comes up out
of the ground in the morning and rises into the sky.

5. Shaping Up

For months I try not drinking so much,
not getting buzzed every day, and get a job
on a Welsh construction site drilling holes
with a jackhammer that later makes me shiver
all night, sitting in a chair listening to music,

watching the electric fire. The police park
outside the door of the house teasing us every day
about the bust they're going to make, and
I've had enough.
I leave the house in Wales, thankful for the breath
and return to New York and try to stay straight.
I go to meetings where people tell me
how it is now they believe they are connected
to themselves, and there's talk of God
that makes me hesitate, but it can't be worse
than all I've believed in.

I go back to shape the union hall and wait
around for weeks to get sent out on a job,
to hoist things, to make something grow. And now
in this Brooklyn neighborhood I walk past early
morning step-sitters flourishing in Spanish,
dark people waiting for a bus, eating fish
outside bodegas. The neighborhood is under
renewal and I feel like I'm being remade
from the inside out. The street by this site
is slit and gutted like an eel, stuffed
with pipes and wires, the arteries of this building,
paved over, driven on by trucks which haul away
the old bits and carry in materials for construction.
And now I have the arms of this machine in my arms,
and we're moving in a rhythm I could get used to.
The bellman rings me from these dreams.
I move the throttle, the gears engage and somewhere
above me, out of my sight, a platform of bricks
and mortar hurtles towards the top. I watch
the cable wrap itself around the drum, powered
by an engine that makes more sense to me now
than anything ever did before.

I know where every bar is in this neighborhood,
every store that sells beer, and sometimes I climb
to the top of the building which next week
will have another story above it, and look down
and wonder if I should fly. Some nights driving

home I squeeze the wheel and start to cry
for the taste that's stronger the salt that runs
down from my cheeks and turns cold above my lips,
and I keep on driving.

3

Home Room

In my dog life I chased my tail,
every chance I got, licked my balls,
booted myself in the ass,
sniffed after every bitch, in heat or not.
Want a bone, Mister? Glass of wine?
someone would offer, and I was gone.
I never learned the names of flowers.
Annuals made me sad, perennials nervous,
rising out of the ground year after year.

You hurtin' my self steam, Mister,
a kid in the front row says.
He had been groping his crotch, telling
his classmates what he had eaten for breakfast.
Fuck off, I want to say, but say instead not
to keep his hands to himself, to keep them
on the desk and do his homework
or I'd pink slip him again.

Fat geese dillydally as I leave my work
at work, maunder around the parking lot
looking for my car. Oh God, I fumble,
not again. And not again, again.
Some days, all you can do is sing
and hope the gods don't hear you.
I finally find my vehicle, turn over the engine,
press myself into gear, and try to remember
the various ways to drive myself home.

Picture Day

Indian girl who has a cast
around her arm because,
she says, she fell down the stairs
of the motel her family runs.

Five boys who speak no English
despite the fact that English
is the official language of their African nation,
and the one girl from the same place
who manages to say over and over, Help me!

Girl whose mother dies,
whose father throws away all her photos,
even those in the girl's wallet,
then throws away the notebook
the girl writes elegies in to remember her.

Boy repeating the year for the third
time who will never pick up his pictures,
found a month from now,
shot to death in a parked car.

Tiny girl pregnant with her third child
that will spill out of its embryonic fluid
a half developed image, disappearing
before counting its second breath.

Girl whose parents drive her to church
three nights a week, who with her two older sisters,
slips out of the house and disappears.

Pakistani boy who carries a box cutter,
he says to the police after opening
the neck of an enemy, for sharpening his pencils
like he does at home.

Girl as wide as three girls who refuses
to get in line, who says she don't want
no pictures, who says no one can't make her.

Their teacher the third week of school,
clutching his roll book, trying to learn their names,
standing in line behind them wearing his one new tie.

Passing Period

Traffic is heavy in the hallway
as gawky backpacks drive themselves
from choir to swimming,
history to French, TV Prod to anatomy,
while others head to Test Prep
where their eyes are dotted by drills
as their teacher recalls Wordsworth
was why she studied Lit, not which choices
could be easily eliminated.

Entering the lunchroom, students study
cause and effect when a girl grabs a Snapple
bottle by its fat neck, breaks it on a wall
and scrapes it across the cheek
of another. The students read the lesson
carved onto the girl's face, note the flicker
in her eyes, the blush spilling onto her shoulder
brushed by a teacher who tries to catch her
as she falls.

Free Lunch

Stop the hatin' mister
white man this kid says
trying to cut in line,
but I don't respond
as I corral him and others
from cheating.
Stop the hatin',
he says again, and then,
You won't let me in
'cause I'm black!
I say, the kids you are trying to gyp
are black too, but he repeats,
Stop the hatin' mister
white man, Stop the hatin'
as he drifts to the end
of the line which disappears
on the horizon: an infinity
of hungry children rattling
their way to the counter
where an anonymous matron
dishes out what has been prepared
for them on small styrofoam trays.

Journal

1

Yesterday was havoc & projects
The whole day was fights & shots fired

        Yesterday I stayed home
        & at night went to the drive and ate

Yesterday was locked up for fighting
So I was just thinking of coming home

        Yesterday I stayed over these girls crib
        & just made cream all day

Yesterday I went to the hospital
To see my mom who is very sick

        It was very boring yesterday but
        I managed to get mines

Spreading love a every day thing
For me with the honeys

        It's like the wolf howling at the moon
        Like its groan when comes to cream

Yesterday I got bulled
So I had to clear all that up

        Yesterday I just cold creamed all day

2

Incarcerated
Out of population
Soup & cheese
Too much dressing

       A new chapter
       Guidelines
       Tired of these pigs

I housed all day
Still feeling it
Snow took over
Kept it real

       We loss
       Thinking we were winners

One
More
Year

3

Yesterday was very
Boring but I managed

       All I have to say is spring
       Loving the sound of it

Yesterday I had a good day
With the help of the word very

Progress Report: Atlantic City

One of my students rushes into my room at the Open House
to see if his parents had been there. No, I say, and he yells,
Damn it! They told me they were coming.
What startles me is his voice. For two months he sits
there quietly failing. I hadn't noticed that I'd never heard
him speak till then, till he ran in to check on his folks
who told him they were going to school to see
how he was doing. What gets me is not that he's here
on parent night, but that he knew his wouldn't show up.
He says they like the casinos. This has happened before.

In this latitude where even hurricanes become disorganized
before slamming into shore, there is no barrier to retard
the unnatural disasters spun into motion. The odds plunge
like high school students dropping out of class, like chips
falling between cracks in the boardwalk where a family squats
in the summer, having rented their home to tourists who've come
to game. They live under wood through Labor Day, then emerge
to cheer the Miss America photo-op down the runway.
And one morning on the beach, a contestant tosses a Frisbee
through the foam, blinds the camera with her beautiful, capped teeth,
finds the corpse of a drifter under a lifeguard boat.

Expression

After class I call her up to my desk.
I want to go over your essay, I say.
Her eyes lower to her paper where my red comments
have left welts. I am trying she says.
I just don't know what you are looking for.
I say, Get out what's inside you.
Show more of yourself.
Be honest.
As she leans over my desk I see her breasts
held in a white bra.
I know I shouldn't look in that open blouse.
I should turn my head, avert my eyes,
stand up. However,
I know what I am looking for.
After talking, she nods,
collects her things, ready
to head for another class, another teacher.
I tell her Try harder. Do it over
and show it to me again,
tomorrow.

Chemical Imbalance

Another day on the wing
for the depressed, where vivacious doctors
        watch you shuffle from one uneaten meal

to another, as they try to match
        the elusive elements that will make you
    want to live.

    There is a history in the genes
            that ignores all love.
When the *Times* says even shyness is a trait

        that resists conditioning,
    what hope is there for those
who back away from life

as if it were a fire?
        What hope, when what blazes
            above scorches the clarity of daylight

    into the translucent thickness of ozone?
The superfluous molecule chokes
        the air we must breathe to live.

13th Step

The men I meet here smoke a lot
and are nervous from caffeine and desire
to regenerate their lives.

They talk of waking naked on the lawn,
climbing in bed with daughters, punching
a hand through a mirror.

I want these men the way they want me,
though I'm told, *you don't come to these meetings*
to get laid . . . 'cause you'll only get fucked.

All their stories are one story, my story,
and when I try to utter it my tongue breaks
like glass, and my words spill over it

slowly, sticking like moist blood.
Some nights when I feel myself wanting
too much, I cling to the sheets of my bed

so I don't throw myself through a window.
And in the morning, looking out, I think
it may shape up to be a day worth living.

I leave my room hoping I'll meet a man
who'll not drag me into his own dark mood,
and maybe, I think, I'll begin to spit out the taste.

Basic Skills

When test scores fell at the school for whores
administrators shuffled their excuses,
pushed the staff to teach from bell to bell.
The faculty put their noses to the bedposts,
gave more homework, graded harder,
detained after hours their feckless pupils.
Nothing worked.
There was gum chewing in *Fellatio*,
cold hands in *Fondling*.
They did not concentrate in *Fantasy*,
and were sloppy in *Seduction*.
They talked too loudly during the *Practicum
on Public Places*, pushed when they should
have pulled and didn't take seriously the practice
johns who complained despite discounted fees.
It's not our fault, a teacher whined,
that the students are unmotivated.
They spend too much time in front of the TV.
They are not as prepared as they used to be,
said another. And where are the parents?
A lot of this stuff they should have learned at home.

High School B.C.

Before Columbine
boys could draw
stick figure warriors
blowing each other up
with engorged guns,
and girls could intimidate
their enemies, I'll kill
that tight ass bitch!
And if anyone noticed,
a glare from the teacher
who might even say, Rasheedah!
and Rasheedah would get it,
mumble, I'm sorry
or My bad, or protest—
Did you hear what *she* said?
and it would be over.

Now the students file
through electronic arches
that frisk their bodies
with magnetic fingers
buzzing confidently
for zippers and jewelry,
as insensitive as security's hands
that grope through backpacks,
pawing their gym shorts and text books,
binders and tampons.
Administrators conclude
the students are safe
as Rasheedah wonders in history
why those white boys go berserk,
why they shoot everyone in sight.
She says, if they lived where I live
they would be happy just to be alive.

Separation of Powers

World hunger is breaking out
all over the United States
from the front tiers
to the last rows of this classroom,
where no rose is plucked
until it withers.
In the commonwealth
of privilege, I xerox geniuses
who believe nothing
happens unless they are present.
They have surrendered
popular sovereignty
to an expanding few
and leave no turn unstoned
in this land of good and plenty.
"Anger is a gift," one has carved
into the skin of a desk.
I open to the account
from the Lodz Ghetto
where Rumkowski,
The King of the Jews, proclaims,
"Nothing bad will happen
to people of good will,"
where he promises
to the not yet deported,
"We are on the threshold
of very best times."
The students stir—one raises
his hand, asks if any of this
is going to be on the final.

The Exchange

We spent a year getting to know Jian Min who wouldn't
let me open a door, no matter how many heavy books he carried.
He called me Professor, though I was and am not,
just a teacher like himself at work within these ancient bricks.
And he thanked me every day for words, and bowed his head
and learned to shake my hand. Words, he said, that fell
on his soil and rooted. Words like *God* he was surprised
could be so beautiful and complex, having drunk Mao and Marx
from infant milk. Words like *Glory* could make his face break
into syllables of delight. Forgetting once, I asked how many
children; he said the three words quietly, *One son, six,*
and loved my daughter as if she were his own and gave her gifts,
small paper dolls of horses, birds and fish.

All week that June, we worried him to stay. We knew his life
would never be as safe, infected by our comfort and our things.
How could he succumb after living in this autonomy?
How could that head-hold last once it fell for our terrible,
abrasive liberty? He learned the privilege to talk
wrong and loud, to say what he wanted to say and not duck
the ubiquitous rifle shot.

After the flower held up a tank, after the battle
of the university came and went, after the plaza
was covered with flies, and the poets fled and the slanted
cries of the wretched old men condemned themselves
to death, we tried to keep Jian Min from natural despair.
He was cursed that what he knew he could never forget,
by the fear that he would spread the tragedy of ideas,
which seemed more terrible after the shots on the square.
His eyes had seen the story on TV.
His ears were stung by the generous reports which could prolong
his visa and his life, but when he called the village phone and spoke
with his wife, she said the words, *Jian Min, you must come home now,*
and he did.

The Performance

When the biology professor came to lecture the class
of substance abusers, he brought with him
a smelly bucket of human brains to use as a prop.
Firm as small basketballs bloated with formaldehyde,
the brains swarmed together in their sea of preservatives.
When the professor picked one up and passed it
around, some refused to touch it, backed away
as if they would catch on fire.
When he lifted another that was slit in half, he joked
about schizophrenia, got serious about trauma,
strokes, other accidents that shut down the traffic
between the two hemispheres.

The students were quiet, sober. Even the shortest
attention span endured the lecture, absorbed the warnings.
When he asked for questions, the students said nothing.
The brains were also silent, exhausted from their day at school.
They wanted nothing but to drift like fat carp.
No more handling by the living, the at risk, the addicted.
They wanted to be left alone, to kick off their shoes,
to have a brewskie, and go back to sleep.

School

She makes it through history before her water breaks
in science, is refused a pass, so she runs
to the girls' room with the teacher chasing,
calling for security.

Giving birth in a corridor, she can't be moved,
so they hold the bell to keep the hallway traffic
from grid-locking around her.
There are fights that want to break out
that will have to wait, and drills
and quizzes and experiments with fire,
and the rolling tongues of thirty odd languages.
The pressure of blood surges through arteries
as the load listens to gravity, drops
from the girl's belly.

She lies on the floor while a tribe of administrators
holds her hand, braces her head, catches the crown
of this new child that they must take in,
who has shown up crying, unregistered, and without ID.

The Student

Ming Li and I are sipping tea
in my neglected garden
when I ask if her family
is religious. Just me, she says.
Buddhist?
Yes.

Talk turns to her Taiwanese father
who is difficult. Not just traditional,
she says, but violent and insane.
Who burns her poems.
Who removed the photos
of her mother from her wallet
the day after she died
and burned them too.

I slipped out today, she says,
when he went to the casino.
If he finds out he will beat me.

Silent, we are distracted
by the chorus of bees
working the fuschia
which are unable to raise
their multicolored heads
above their knees.

A gnat lands on my wrist.
I go to swat it.
Careful, she says,
catching my hand,
holding it back.
It could be your mother!

4

The Desire

Last night I dreamt I was drinking again
and got drunk, and walked out on the quiet life
I've been living these last few years.
I watched as I let my family go—
The wife who understood and would not forgive,
The child who clung to my loose clothing, crying
Don't go, Daddy don't go, take Mommy and me
with you.
I remember saying that too, grabbing the coat
of my own father as he swung his arms around
to touch me. And I trailed him
as he followed his father until I let go.

I fell back into sleep, into dreams—
There were rivers I had to cross and recross,
and fires starting in every forest I came to,
and cars screeching around corners,
about to go off a cliff,
about to crash in a desert
where I am thirsty all the time.

A Story About the Father

School was safe until he fell
through the empty pay envelope
he had to fill working the docks on 12th Avenue.
Bananas were the worst!
Many legs crawled out of the hands
he hauled on his bony shoulders.
You've seen *On the Waterfront*?
It was like that until Hitler ate Poland
and France, then reached for Britain.
And that's where we find him,
in a port city in Wales where he loads
ships for D-Day. Walking the damp streets
he gives in to the music wafting from a pub
where the barmaid ignores him
long enough to fall in love, get the ring,
then kiss him off when his wave crashes
at Omaha, late and safe, then on to Belgium
to unload more ships that feed the invasion.
A buddy steals a jeep loaded with whiskey,
picks him up and crashes it on the long road out of town.
Found by MP's who steal again the cargo
and leave them in ditches.
When he wakes in starched sheets,
a doctor stings with good news, *You're going home.*
No, no, he says, thinking of the labor
he would have or not have, the hands
blistering his shoulders, pressing its many fingers
deep into the fault lines of his skin.
Don't be a hero, son, the doctor ordered.
You're going home.

The Commuting

My father, retired in Florida,
hallowed out a life in the dark
tunnels beneath Manhattan, plummeting
fifty years to jobs that despised him.
He raised buildings out of holes
dug many stories beneath ground level.
On the A Train, he tore away pages of the paper-
covered books as he read them—Mailer, Bellows,
Roth—books which illuminated the descent.
And twice each month he'd rail back into Manhattan
to the philharmonic to listen to his symphonies.

I had never dwelled in my father's house
until I listened to Mozart's 36th, the first movement
of the Linz, where the strings and the winds converge
on one dark corner, where wood and gut and polished metal
and the percussionous air from inside the body
escape in one gush, one enormous breath.
Then light. Ferocious light. Enough to read by.
Enough to see him home.

The Lesson

Years before my brother left his horrible body
the virus had loved too much, we found him
playing in the street, reaching out between parked cars
sticking an arm, then a leg, into the mouth of traffic.
After the shout and the terror-quick slap to his bottom,
our father tried to explain what it means to die.

He said in a calmness I'd never heard before
or since, When you're dead, you'll be the little boy
who doesn't come around anymore. And Eddie,
who liked to play in the street, who didn't care
that he was slapped, who liked to stick things
where they did not belong, he heard him,
and he blinked, and for years
I thought he had listened.
I thought he understood.

Last Words

for Eddie

We thought the hallucinogenic wandering
he did was drug induced, that the date he had with Rita
Hayworth, *You know who Rita Hayworth is, don't you?*
and the names he gave his small herd of soft, toy cows
were shot from the trajectory of some powerful narcotic
used to keep him comfortable.
But then we learned it was the stem of his brain
rotting like some old tree; that the virus had camped
there while reconnoitering the rest of the brain,
having already taken the lungs, filling them with fluid
on its campaign to surround the heart.

Does the virus live on in the body once it has killed it?
Are there words to describe this subversion, the urge
to consume what for so long has held it aloft?

The last words I heard him utter still pour in,
unlike the rhythmic dripping of his fluids and breaths.
What we were all praying for before it came,
he said as clearly as an anchorman, *I'm trying to turn
it off!*

Questions

for Stephen Dunn

My tongue rubs itself
against the resonance
of abstract words
whose syllables nudge
the flesh and bones
of consciousness
to pronounce
the unknowable.
A sun whose light
dazzles so we only see
this world where want is.
You call it a leap,
and I agree, like
the imagination that spells
the truth of poems.
Evil is a turning away,
suffering intended
so our bodies learn to trudge
on knees and elbows,
while our faces facing
the earth lift like heliotropes
toward the awesome.

My name is Peter, petros, rock—
a lexicon of doubt
and betrayal, a fashioning
of molecules beaten
by invisible gusts that raze
my sandstone face
from the rough host
of its body and send it
swirling into the source
of the sky. I can't see it,
good friend, but I know
it's there.

Breakfast at the Wildwood Motel

Last night when I entered this city without reservations
I got lost in its wailing as fire trucks crawled
along Ocean Avenue for the Halloween Parade.
I was caught between engines and couldn't turn
as children jumped in the street to gather candy
tossed by goblins driving the huge rigs.
At a convenience store, Satan the clerk gave me
directions and I followed them. It's always open,
he said, even when no one is there.

I sit in a booth by a window. My dirty plate screams
of gluttony—smeared yolks, crust of rye toast,
home fries, resonance of ketchup.
A blind man taps into the coffee shop, sits
at the counter. Waitress sings, Good Morning, Doctor!
Brings him a horseradish omelet.
Rubber bats float from a slow ceiling fan.
In the window, Santa's elves retooled with axes
hack at the head of a Barbie doll. On the soundtrack—
Guns 'N Roses warble "O Holy Night."
The blind man stabs his fork into his breakfast.
The waitress returns with coffee.
Outside the ocean churns.
Small ghosts dressed like children
knock at the motel door, beg for sweets, beg for someone
to let them in, each of them opening and closing his hands.

Manifesto

I do not do nature.
It hurts too much.
Pricklies along
that country road
you call quaint.
I burn my feet
on the razor sand
by the ocean
that roars all night
down the block
from my sleep.
How does anything get
done when you're out
there picking flowers,
petting dogs, staring
at stars that clutter
the night sky?
Nah, give me a home
without buffalo and cows
and trees that annoy
with their loud branches
scratching the panes
of my well-insulated house.
Give me my Subaru,
which I drive to the office,
windows rolled up
in the comfort
of conditioned air.
Give me convenience stores
with serve-yourself coffee,
creamers, and sugared flares
that light up the sky
under my chin
with their powdery explosives.
Give me liberty to commute
from one video store

to the next to track down
The Gods Must Be Republicans,
which I will view
without you
from the comfort
of my vinyl love seat,
a bowl of popped corn,
a can of birch beer,
my corpulent fingers
grazing the well-
appointed features
of the remote.

The Toast

    Do not throw the soft bodies of rice
at these we love. Instead, pelt them
        with rocks. Scar their smooth skins

    with the sharpest stones.
        Make the groom bleed and the bride weep.
May they never forget this reception

        in honor of their lives together.
May they learn that when one wears clothing
    that catches on fire, the other must beat them

to save them from burning.

Changing the Light

My daughter's flickering bulb has not yet dropped
its useful filament which stutters
        then sparks up her room just fine.

        So I tell her when she nags, Be patient.
It's not yet time to unclasp the fixture. Soon
        the room will go dark as a storm

        and then I will come with the chair from
                the living room and a bulb from the closet
and stand in the center and raise my arm

toward the ceiling and touch what she cannot yet touch, take it
        in my fingers and turn it backwards,
                then wind in the fresh one which spits on,

        and I will notice how her shape has rounded
        since the last bulb blew, how gorgeous and full
of light she has become

as she turns in her bed towards the wall.

The Formality

At the Eighth Grade Prom which I got suckered into chaperoning
the pubescent couples arrive in stretch limos that let them out
in the playground near the swings and teeter board.
The girls in expensive gowns stutter on heels, click their gum,
their heads molded in permanent waves, dips, storms, beehives,
honey dos, as their corsaged breasts swell and flower.
One strikes a Madonna pose, pushes herself up
as if it were the next day and the asphalt were a beach
blanket and she, the darling fun girl surrounded by bronze brutes,
each begging her to save the last wave for him.

Inside, the gym is a jungle of crepe paper which the boys drag down
to strip the balloons from their branches and put them in their mouths,
sucking helium to make their transparent voices whistle like cartoon drunks.
They hijack a cooler of coke and shake the cans before popping
them open to spray themselves and their dates whose satin dresses stain
like wounds. One young lady chases them over the tables, screams
I'll kill you, you scum sucking douche bags! while the principal gladhands
the parents who have come to tape their new men and women.

If only my daughter were not part of this. Streaming from one ring
to another, whispering among the princesses, converging on the tribe
of boys—she gestures to the one who wears his cap backwards,
the one whose dirt brown shirt comes loose from his pants
as they begin to move to the hip hop, as they wrap themselves
in its icy tubes of war music. I see how he looks her over,
how his eyes say Me hungry, as he jumps up and down
before her polished smile. Other bodies follow them into the whirl
beneath the mock chandelier which twists the spotted light
and fractures it over their bodies as they rock their heads,
stretch their arms toward the flashing sky, open their mouths
as if to inhale, as if to shout, as if to taste the honey of their June-new flesh.

The Gap

Time waits for no man, I remind my daughter.
O, I am sure he waits for his wife, she retorts,
snapping her clever tongue like a jump rope.
It used to be that I was the quick one.
Now this child with thin, athletic legs
which balance the makings of a woman,
has leaped ahead. Time wounds all healing,
she says, and she's right. The last time I dribbled
a basketball my knees hurt for two months.
Don't worry, she says, soon you'll be dribbling
without trying.

It no longer hurts to say what I said I would never say,
exploding into her blasted room. Turn that music down!
But Daddy, it's the Beatles!
I don't care! and I don't, knowing the Earth
just sprung from the orbit it's revolved around
since the Sixties.

The sun moves quietly in this winter sky, quietly
and slow, its brief show more sketch than performance.
All things must pass to come again, and I spin Louie
and Ella on the turntable. They swing so fairly, so evenly,
even I can catch it, as she dances out of her crib
dressed for the elements in boxer shorts, tights, plaid Converse,
lumberjack flannel shirt. She sings along, Birds do it. Bees do it.
I'm going out so you and mommy can do it . . . But I'm ready
this time, snap her off her feet, wrap her in my arms, dance
her to the foyer. I plant my lips on her lips,
Forties movie style, look into her startled eyes, and slow,
beautifully slow, open the front door and put her out
until curfew.

The Planets

My daughter has been complaining that our house
is an anachronism, that we're like totally out of touch.
She lists The Best of our shortcomings—No
microwave, No clothes dryer, No dishwasher,
No answering machine, No air conditioner, and on.
You're techno-phobic, she tells me, an embarrassment
to your generation and to my own. No way! I protest,
pointing to the color TV, the VCR. Please, she argues,
there's no remote. They aren't even cable ready.

Returning late from the mall, she waves off my inquisition
with a disc gleaming in holographic light, and places it
into a borrowed CD Man. I hear the strains of "Jupiter"
burst from her head, Gustav Holst's The Planets, and wonder
how that god felt when Athena sparkled out of his skull.
I wonder too at the articulate rebelliousness
of this noisy girl listening to the music
of the spheres that wraps around her, this planet
who cannot help but return after spinning so far away
in her revolutions around the Sun.

Physics

The size of the universe expands, she tells me,
not as I had expected, spilling its matter

into another universe on the other side.
But the bodies within it drift

imperceptibly apart within the star-dazzled dark.
I tell her, I get it, I think.

We stand our own organic molecules
upright on terra firma, but do not notice

or protest that every beeping thing,
even love, is moving us apart.

Intensive Care in Atlantic City

You were too breathless in Emergency to cry
when they whirled me into machines that measured
my beat and counted the enzymes in my blood.
And like most things this way, the results were ambiguous,
both dying and living, gray, like the ashen face
you saw through your silver-blue eyes.

How you rubbed your hands where my heart once beat
strong, then hugged my dizzy head against your chest,
against the rules of the heart wing, and our daughter
laughed for the first time that week, when she saw
the green blip on the monitor jump quickly
in the night colored screen.

You were determined to learn how to breathe with me
at the stress clinic, that we would go it together.
In through the nose, holding it in, spilling it out the mouth.
How you squeezed my hand, hurting it, when the psychologist
stuttered and passed out, the victim of a job he loved
too much, like my heart in the middle of its sentence,
in the middle of its beautiful, bloody vocation.

Before leaving the hospital, you took notes on what's to go
into my mouth, more important they warned, than what comes out.
And I protested, My body's too greedy! But they nagged me
before letting me go, and I clung to you as they wheeled me
towards Park Place. That's when we saw the two falcons
pull out over the gaming halls—past Caesars, past Trump,
past the abandoned Dunes—a pair of them reclaiming
this city, drifting silently out to sea.

The Painters

You were surprised to find me in the basement
when you came down to do laundry.
I was hiding from the painters and the heat
lying on the floor with my hands
behind my head, thinking of nothing.
I saw you look out a window at the gritty knees
and splattered shoes of the outside crew.
And we both could hear the inside men
upstairs moving their rollers up and down
against the walls.
You hesitated, then put down your dirty work
and joined me on that floor.
How pleased we were by this—the busy men
outside moving ladders, tying back bushes
and trees, and above us, the placing
of drop-cloths on the furniture—so much
going on around us and soon even our cutoffs
were too much to wear.
When the heat went down we went upstairs
to the new walls of our old surroundings.
Our love-sweat mixed with the smell
of the paint. It was a place we left
not long ago and had come back to,
but better than we remembered.
We didn't know then that our daughter
was conceived, how the mixing of liquids
inside you could produce such brightness.
And outside, the foreman waited for us
in his truck, taking care of invoices,
figuring out his next job, estimates
for the future.

Acknowledgments

The following poems have been published or are forthcoming, sometimes in different versions, in these journals:

The Beloit Poetry Journal – "The Formality," "Shaping Up," "The Stubborn Child"
Common Journeys – "Last Words"
Confrontation – "The Commuting"
The Cortland Review – "Baptism"
CQ (California State Poetry Quarterly) – "Intensive Care in Atlantic City"
Cottonwood – "Physics"
Edison Review – "Underemployment"
The Journal of New Jersey Poets – "The Exchange," "The Healing," "The Judgment,"
    "The Neighborhood"
LIPS – "The Planets"
Many Mountains Moving – "Questions"
Mediphors – "The Lesson"
Natural Bridge – "A Story About the Father"
The New York Quarterly – "Expression," "Sequence"
Passages North – "The Painters"
Poets On – "Changing The Light," "The Toast"
The Quarterly – "Fishing," "Heavy Construction," "Why I Am Not a Catholic"
Spelunker Flophouse – "School"
U.S. 1 Worksheets – "The Narrows," "13th Step"
Without Halos – "The Desire"
Witness – "The Performance"
Yellow Silk – "The Bridge"

"Chemical Imbalance" appears courtesy of *Commonweal*, © 2004 Commonweal Foundation. Reprinted with permission (www.commonweal-magazine.org). "Oreo" and "Passing Period" appear courtesy of *English Journal*, © 2001 by the National Council of Teachers of English. Reprinted with permission. "The Toast" was reprinted in *The New York Times*. "The Narrows" was reprinted in *Slipstream*.

In addition, the following poems have been printed or reprinted in these anthologies:

"The Painters" – *Anthology of Magazine & Yearbook of American Poetry*, 1988
"Changing the Light," "The Toast" – *Anthology of Magazine & Yearbook of American Poetry*, 1997
"The Formality" – *Essential Love* (Grayson Books)
"Intensive Care in Atlantic City"– *Findings* (Atlantic City Medical Center)
"Sequence," "Learning to Swim at Poverty Beach" – *Never Before: Poems About First Experiences* (Four Way Books)

"The New Boy"– *Outsiders: Poems about Rebels, Exiles, and Renegades* (Milkweed Editions)

"The Painters" – *Passages North Anthology* (Milkweed Editions)

"The Stubborn Child" – *Poets & Prophets - Selected Poems* (Poets & Prophets)

"Breakfast at the Wildwood Motel" – *Shore Stories: Tales of the Jersey Shore* (Down the Shore Publishing)

"The Desire," "Sobriety," "The Stubborn Child" – *Sixteen Voices: Survivors of Incest & Sexual Abuse* (Mariposa Publishing)

"Why I Am Not a Catholic" – *Speaking Our Truth* (Harper-Collins)

"Progress Report: Atlantic City" – *Under a Gull's Wing: Poetry of the Jersey Shore* (Down the Shore Publishing)

"Manifesto" – *Urban Nature: Poems About Wildlife in the City* (Milkweed Editions)

"The Desire," "The Narrows," "The Painters," "Shaping Up" (Part 5) – *Voices From A Borrowed Garden* (Buffalo Press)

"The Bridge" – *Yellow Silk: Erotic Arts and Letters* (Harmony Books)